AGE OF DINOSAURS: **STEGOSAURUS**

AGE OF DINOSAURS:

Stegosaurus

SHERYL PETERSON

CREATIVE EDUCATION

Published by Creative Education
P.O. Box 227, Mankato, Minnesota 56002
Creative Education is an imprint of The Creative Company
www.thecreativecompany.us

Design and production by Blue Design
Art direction by Rita Marshall
Printed by Corporate Graphics in the United States of America

Photographs by Alamy (Imagery and Imagination, Wendy
White), Bridgeman Art Library (English Photographer, English
School, Arthur Oxenham, Roger Payne), Corbis (Louie Psihoyos,
Paul A. Souders), Getty Images (DEA Picture Library, Wolfgang
Kaehler, Ken Lucas), iStockphoto (Linda Bucklin, Franky De
Meyer, David Parsons, Mickaël Plichard), Library of Congress,
Sarah Yakawonis/Blue Design

Library of Congress Cataloging-in-Publication Data
Peterson, Sheryl.
Stegosaurus / by Sheryl Peterson.
p. cm. — (Age of dinosaurs)
Summary: An introduction to the life and era of the armor-
plated, herbivorous dinosaur known as Stegosaurus, starting
with the creature's late-1800s discovery and ending with
present-day research topics.
Includes bibliographical references and index.
ISBN 978-1-58341-976-2
1. Stegosaurus—Juvenile literature. I. Title. II. Series.

QE862.065P48 2010
567.915'3—dc22   2009025176

CPSIA: 120109 PO 1089

First Edition
9 8 7 6 5 4 3 2 1

CONTENTS

STEGOSAURUS TALES

ROOF-PLATED LIZARD

In 1886, in a dusty sandstone quarry near Cañon City, Colorado, a farmer named Marshall P. Felch worked slowly and carefully. He chipped at and scraped away layers of the hard stone, hoping to discover another fossil or dinosaur bone. Felch had been digging in this quarry for years, and after digging all day in the hot sun, he often had only a few fragments of a skeleton to show for his efforts. But following his employer's instructions, he retrieved every piece, no matter how tiny.

From about 1883 to 1890, Felch worked for one of the most famous **paleontologists** of the 19th century, Othniel Charles (O. C.) Marsh. He was paid about $85 a month to unearth prehistoric fossils in his quarry, pack the bones and fossils embedded in blocks of cemented sandstone carefully in large wooden crates, and send them by train to the East Coast. Marsh wrote letters of advice to Felch and waited in his office at Yale College for shipments. When the crates arrived, the scientist would sort the petrified bones, group them by animal, and possibly record a new **species** name.

The first stegosaur species had already been found in 1877 by English clergyman Arthur Lakes, who was looking for fossilized leaves and instead found dinosaur bones in the Morrison Formation, an outcropping of rock from the Late Jurassic Period located in Colorado, Wyoming, and Utah. Lakes then sent a box of bones to Marsh. After much research, Marsh introduced the new dinosaur to the world as

Once paleontologists collected enough bones to be able to reconstruct dinosaurs such as *Stegosaurus*, artists helped them picture the rest.

Stegosaurus armatus, from the family Stegosauridae and the order Ornithischia (which means "bird-hipped").

The name *Stegosaurus* was derived from the Greek words *stegos* ("roof") and *sauros* ("lizard"), which described the bony, kite-shaped plates that jutted up from the creature's neck, back, and upper tail. Marsh originally thought that the plates lay flat over the animal's back, overlapping like shingles on a roof. The paleontologist surmised that the creature had lived 154 to 144 million years ago in the Late Jurassic Period of the Mesozoic Era, the age of dinosaurs.

However, since the *Stegosaurus* found by Lakes was missing many parts, including a skull, Marsh hired Felch to help him find a complete skeleton. From 1883 to 1886, Felch dug up dinosaur bones that all seemed to be from the same unique beast. He uncovered diamond-shaped plates that appeared to jut out from the animal's backbone. During this time, Felch recovered more than 200 related bones, including tail bones with spikes. He found everything except the most important part—the dinosaur's head.

Felch often tried to hire extra men to help him dig. However, as he claimed in a letter to Marsh, he could not get hired hands to be interested in any bone smaller than a barn door. Felch's young daughter Sarah grew curious, though, and used her artistic skills to sketch the fossils as they were retrieved. Often it was necessary to remove huge chunks of rock to find even a small fossil. In Felch's words, "It is like dislodging an enemy from a strongly fortified position, and we must take the fortress along with it, all without a scratch."

A native of Massachusetts, Marshall P. Felch worked his way West after serving in the Union Army during the American Civil War (from 1861 to 1865).

Armchair Paleontologist

Paleontologist Othniel Charles Marsh named many dinosaurs, including *Stegosaurus*. Marsh was born in Lockport, New York, on October 29, 1831, and died on March 18, 1899. His mother, Mary, was the younger sister of the millionaire George Peabody, whose wealth and establishment of Yale's Peabody Museum of Natural History enabled Marsh's later success as a scientist. Marsh earned his undergraduate degree from Yale College in 1860 and later returned to become the institution's first professor of vertebrate paleontology. In 1869, Peabody died, and Marsh inherited a sizable fortune that allowed him to continue his dinosaur research. During the next 30 years, Marsh published more than 300 scientific papers in which he described and named roughly 500 new species of fossils. Marsh did not spend much time in the field digging, preferring to research and write instead. Because of this, many scientists referred to Marsh as an "armchair paleontologist." Marsh remains famous for his widely accepted theory that birds evolved from dinosaurs. His vast fossil collections are on display at the Peabody Museum in New Haven, Connecticut, and at the Smithsonian Institution in Washington, D.C.

Paleontologist

O. C. Marsh

N. 7705

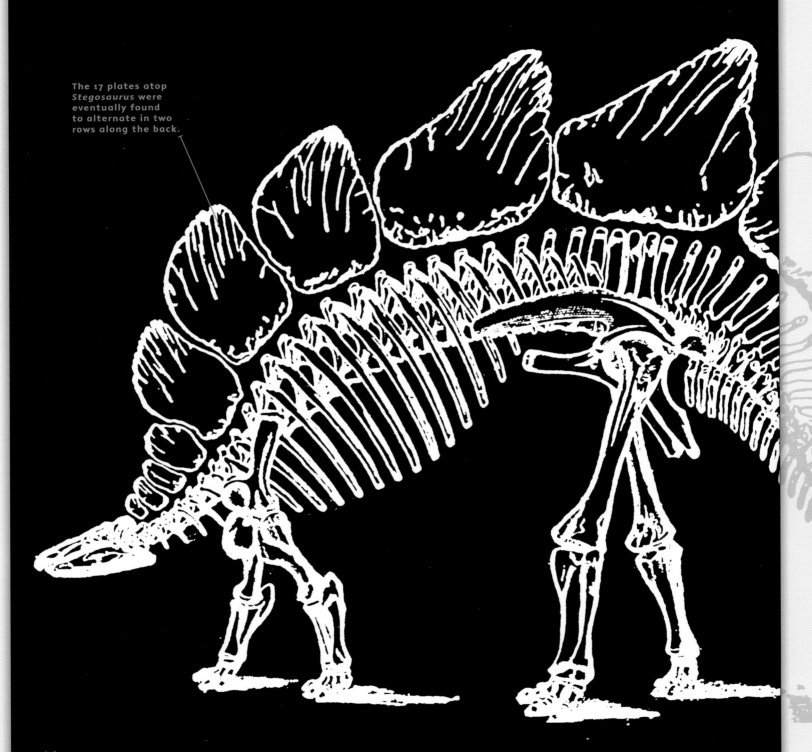

The 17 plates atop *Stegosaurus* were eventually found to alternate in two rows along the back.

One day, Felch's tool struck pay dirt as he dug up a dinosaur skull that appeared to match all the other bones he had been sending out East. The skeleton was complete. Keeping the news to himself, Felch prepared detailed notes about the position of the bones in the land. He packed the fragile skull in soft cotton, placed his treasure inside several cloth bags, and sent it off by rail. When Marsh unpacked the crate, he could not believe his luck. Finally, after 10 years, he had a *Stegosaurus* skeleton, complete with a skull.

Scientists around the world were fascinated by the strange characteristics of *Stegosaurus*. Its small head, armored body, and four tail spikes were unusual, but it was the dinosaur's triangular plates that were truly mysterious. Marsh described them as "a most remarkable feature which could not have been anticipated, and would hardly have been credited had not the plates themselves been found in position."

Marsh named this species *Stegosaurus stenops* and considered it to be closely related to the first specimen he had named. Much later, when the bones were put on display at the Smithsonian National Museum of Natural History in Washington, D.C., the skeleton gained the nickname "Roadkill," since it was laid out just as it had been found and resembled highway roadkill. Over the years, Marsh recovered more than 20 *Stegosaurus* specimens in all, comprising a number of related stegosaurid species.

During the late 1800s, scientists may have been interested in Marsh's finds, but newspapers did not report much about the important fossil

The Bone Wars

At one time, paleontologists O. C. Marsh and Edward Drinker Cope were friends. But after Marsh pointed out that Cope's 1868 reconstruction of *Elasmosaurus* was flawed, with the head placed where the tail should have been, "The Bone Wars" began. The two famous scientists often used underhanded methods to out-compete each other in the fossil fields of the American West. Cope and Marsh hired "dinosaur rustlers" to spy on the competitor's digs, and their workers smashed fossils, dynamited sites so the other couldn't collect from them, and filled in digging sites with rubble when they weren't being used. The two viciously attacked each other in the *New York Herald* and scientific journals in attempts to discredit the other's reputation and cut off his funding. On his deathbed, Cope issued one final challenge to Marsh. Cope donated his brain to science and thought Marsh should do the same. Since at the time it was thought that brain size was the measure of intelligence, Cope wanted both brains measured someday to see who was smarter. However, Marsh never accepted the challenge, and Cope's skull is still preserved at the University of Pennsylvania.

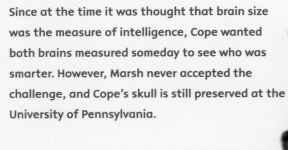

discoveries. Oftentimes, editors made cartoons out of the dinosaur news instead. One 1890s cartoon in the *New York Herald* showed Marsh as a circus ringmaster holding off prehistoric beasts with a whip.

However, a spirited scientific competition raged between Marsh and fellow paleontologist Edward Drinker Cope during the time of the *Stegosaurus* discoveries. This period of intense fossil speculation and discovery in the American West became known as "The Bone Wars." Marsh represented the Yale Peabody Museum, and Cope was a professor at the Academy of Natural Sciences in Philadelphia. From about 1868 to 1892, the two men spent thousands of dollars funding expeditions, hiring bone collectors away from each other, and bidding against each other in a battle of one-upmanship.

European paleontologists were upset by the brash behavior and careless methods of their American counterparts. In the rush to reassemble dinosaurs,

Cope and Marsh were both guilty of substituting parts from different species and misidentifying certain body parts altogether. This sometimes led to misconceptions that lingered for decades.

For the most part, though, this battle between Cope and Marsh helped to feed the American public's appetite for new dinosaurs. Between them, the two men named more than 130 new dinosaur species. Before Cope and Marsh began their research, only 18 dinosaur species were known to North Americans. The two scientists made *Allosaurus*, *Stegosaurus*, and *Triceratops* household names. The reconstructed skeletons slowly but surely made their way to major museums, where most reside to the present day.

From his study (below), Edward Drinker Cope produced more than 1,200 scientific papers, many about reptiles and their ancient ancestors, such as *Stegosaurus*.

WANDERING PLANT-EATER

How did **herbivores** such as *Stegosaurus* get to become some of the most massive animals to ever walk the earth? Most likely, they lumbered around all day in search of fresh leaves and shoots to fuel their hulking frames. *Stegosaurus* would have tromped through western North America's forests of cedar, sequoia, and cypress trees and browsed on low vegetation such as leaves and ferns, which grew in abundance in the humid Jurassic **climate**. Nonflowering horsetails, club mosses, and **conifers** would have been other abundant food sources. *Stegosaurus* did not eat grass, though, because that plant had not yet appeared on Earth.

In comparison with its gigantic body, *Stegosaurus* had a very small, boxlike head that was a little smaller than a modern giraffe's. At the end of its head, the disproportional dinosaur had a horn-covered beak, which it held low to the ground. *Stegosaurus* used its beak to bite off leaves and vegetation before chewing.

When the dinosaur fed, the top and bottom of its snout came together, sharpening the beak's edges against each other. Inside its pouchy cheeks and weak jaws were small, jagged, leaf-shaped teeth. *Stegosaurus* may have loaded its cheeks with plants, then chewed repeatedly to break down the fibers or simply swallowed the

Colorado. The tracks were found by researchers from the Morrison Natural History Museum led by museum director Matthew Mossbrucker and were the first representations of *Stegosaurus* hatchling footprints ever seen. One rock appears to show four or five *Stegosaurus* babies all heading in the same direction. The small 3-toed tracks could be covered by a 50-cent piece, suggesting that the hatchlings were about the size of a newborn human. Mossbrucker noted, "The tracks are so crisply preserved that I can imagine the sound of tiny feet splashing up water when the baby dinosaurs came to this ancient river to drink and cool down." Another boulder includes a partial juvenile hind paw track that was stepped on by an adult *Stegosaurus*, suggesting to scientists that the dinosaurs moved in multi-age herds. Although not everyone is convinced that the tracks indeed belonged to *Stegosaurus*, prominent paleontologist Robert Bakker concurred with Mossbrucker's findings. The fossils are on permanent display at the Morrison Natural History Museum.

plants whole. The dinosaur's digestive system would have extracted nutrients from the partly chewed or unchewed food, eliminating the need for many teeth and strong jaw muscles. Most likely, *Stegosaurus* also swallowed gastroliths, small stones that tumbled around in the dinosaur's stomach to help grind up food. Gastroliths have been found with recent *Stegosaurus* skeletons, and modern **reptiles** such as crocodiles are known to eat rocks to aid in digestion as well.

*S*tegosaurus grew to be the length of a school bus, or about 30 feet (9 m) long, and weighed about 3.4 tons (3 t). Most *Stegosaurus* species were elephant-sized and stood almost 14 feet (4.3 m) high. A quadraped, the big beast walked on all four legs. *Stegosaurus* was very slow-moving and seemed to live a solitary life of continuous eating. No hard evidence has been found to prove *Stegosaurus* lived in herds, but paleontologists have discovered fossil skeletons of many *Stegosaurus* specimens located close together in Utah. That suggests that at least some *Stegosaurus* grazed together, possibly for protection from large meat-eating dinosaurs.

Despite its body's size, the brain of *Stegosaurus* was small, like its head. It was possibly the smallest brain of any dinosaur and, weighing in at 2.8 ounces (80 g), was the size of a walnut or a golf ball. Consequently, as measured by the ratio of its brain to its

body mass, most scientists concluded that *Stegosaurus* was not very smart. Still, the giant, long-necked sauropods such as *Diplodocus* or *Brachiosaurus* are considered to have had even less brain power.

A small brain also usually signals that an animal's reflexes are poor. Fortunately, *Stegosaurus*'s eyes were on the sides of its head, making it easier for the dinosaur to spot approaching predators. Plus, *Stegosaurus* would have relied on its sense of smell to detect danger, not to mention locating the tastiest plants.

The spiky dinosaur supported its weight on strong, pillar-like legs. Its back legs were twice as long as its front legs and ended in padded feet and short toes. Each hind foot had three small toes, while each forefoot had five. Most paleontologists agree that *Stegosaurus* walked slowly on all four legs like an elephant and trotted for short distances. Others believe that *Stegosauru*s was able to rear up and balance on its sturdy tail and hind limbs, forming a tripod, to forage in the crowns of trees like kangaroos.

The showy plating on a *Stegosaurus*'s body was its most recognizable feature. A crest of 17 kite-shaped plates ran the length of its back and tail in what paleontologists now know was a staggered line. Thick, bony calluses called scutes padded the throat and hip area and would have acted as body armor against predators. Millions of years before the **medieval** invention, *Stegosaurus* had its own

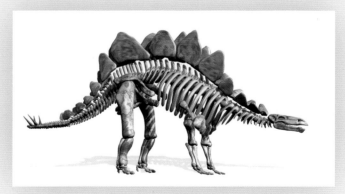

The Thagomizer

Scientists had long known that *Stegosaurus* had spikes at the end of its flexible tail, but the protrusions received a new name in a very unusual manner. In 1982, cartoonist Gary Larson featured the dinosaur in a *Far Side* comic strip in which a caveman professor in a lecture hall points to the spikes on the tail of a large *Stegosaurus*. He explains to his primitive listeners, "Now this end is called the thagomizer ... after the late Thag Simmons." According to Larson's imagination, Thag Simmons was an unfortunate prehistoric human who discovered the dangers of *Stegosaurus*'s tail spikes firsthand—even though the existence of humans during the time of the dinosaurs is contrary to all scientific evidence. However, ever since Larson drew the cartoon that coined the term "thagomizer," the word has been adopted by scientists and institutions alike. The odd nickname was first put into practice by paleontologist Kenneth Carpenter in a 1993 presentation. He may have been joking at the time, but the new name stuck. "Thagomizer" can even be seen on *Stegosaurus* displays at the Smithsonian Institution and the Dinosaur National Monument.

Stegosaurus Defense

Tail Spikes

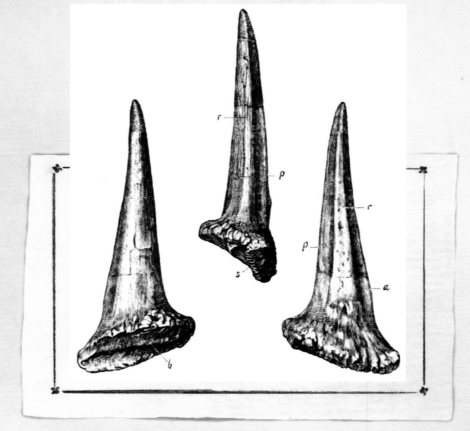

version of **chain mail**, which consisted of a series of bones under its neck that acted as a shield.

The heavy, muscular tail, which arched upward, was *Stegosaurus*'s secret weapon in self-defense. Four solid spikes, known collectively as the thagomizer, each measured two to four feet (.6–1.2 m) long and stuck out from the plated tail. Only the largest **carnivorous** dinosaurs would have risked attacking a full-grown *Stegosaurus*. Even so, a strolling *Stegosaurus* had to be on constant guard against potential threats.

To keep its species alive, *Stegosaurus* laid six or more eggs per **clutch**, covered them with twigs and leaves, and left them buried until they hatched. It is likely that dinosaurs laid their eggs once a year, so a single female dinosaur probably hatched hundreds of babies in her lifetime. Although no *Stegosaurus* eggs have been found to date, dinosaur eggs and **embryos** have been discovered in more than 150 areas around the world, with 37 of those sites being in North America. Most of these eggs are from bipedal theropods—members of a class of meat-eating, predatory dinosaurs that moved on two legs—and date from the Cretaceous Period (144 to 65 million years ago). Paleontologists surmise that *Stegosaurus* eggs would have been similar.

Once hatched, the young probably had to become self-sufficient in a short time in order to survive. Since paleontologists have discovered full-grown dinosaur fossils near eggs and juveniles, they theorize that most dinosaurs took care of their young much like modern birds do, by watching over their nests and bringing food to the new hatchlings.

Paleontologist Jack Horner is well known for his discoveries of dinosaur eggs in Montana, some containing fossilized skeletons of embryos.

WARM JURASSIC HOME

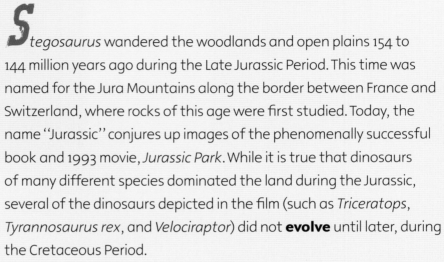

*S*tegosaurus wandered the woodlands and open plains 154 to 144 million years ago during the Late Jurassic Period. This time was named for the Jura Mountains along the border between France and Switzerland, where rocks of this age were first studied. Today, the name "Jurassic" conjures up images of the phenomenally successful book and 1993 movie, *Jurassic Park*. While it is true that dinosaurs of many different species dominated the land during the Jurassic, several of the dinosaurs depicted in the film (such as *Triceratops*, *Tyrannosaurus rex*, and *Velociraptor*) did not **evolve** until later, during the Cretaceous Period.

During *Stegosaurus*'s lifetime, Earth was a very different place. Scientists believe that most of Earth's landmasses, now called continents, were clumped together into one giant supercontinent called Pangaea. During the 64 million years of the Jurassic, the supercontinent broke into two major fragments—Laurasia in the north and Gondwana in the south—and the continents of North America and South America drifted farther apart from Europe and Africa. As the continents moved, they collided with pieces of the ocean floor, causing the formation of several mountain ranges around the world—including the Rocky Mountains in North America and the Alps in Europe.

Climates changed in different parts of the world as the landmasses moved to different areas, but the overall climate became warmer and

Museums such as the Smithsonian Insitution's National Museum of Natural History showcase models of Jurassic creatures such as *Stegosaurus*.

DO NOT TOUCH

The meat-eating
Ceratosaurus
(opposite), which had
a short horn on its
snout, was a likely
predator of the plant-
eating *Stegosaurus*.

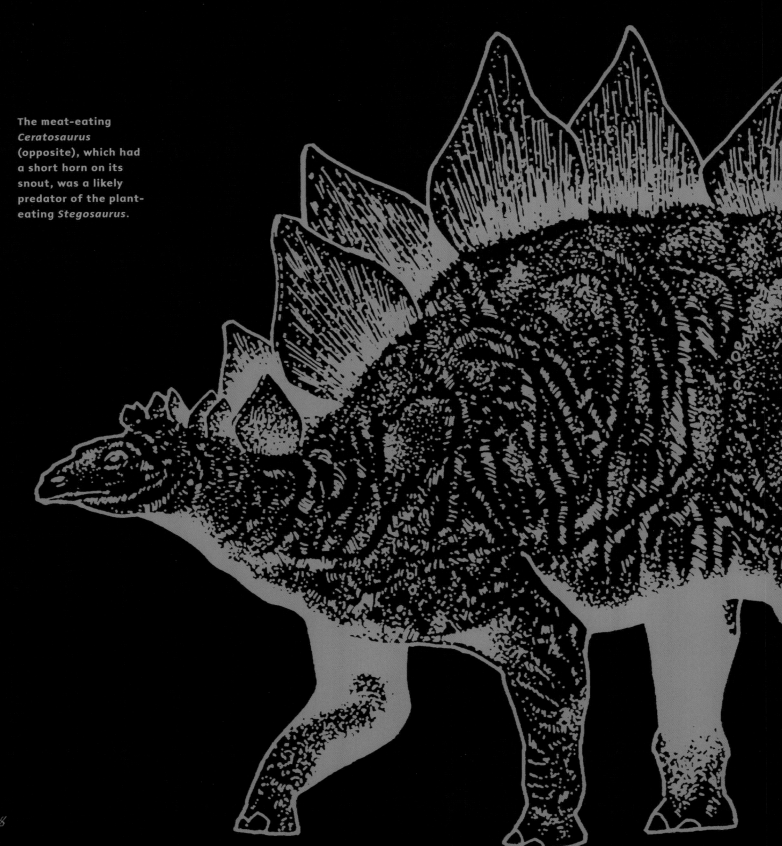

more humid, allowing jungles to grow and cover much of the land. At the North and South poles, the air was cool but not cold. Monsoon conditions occurred across some lowland regions, creating wide river basins that were prone to flash floods. This, in turn, gave rise to vast flooded plains that returned much moisture into the air, supporting abundant plant life.

Jurassic forests were home to a number of early **mammals** no bigger than rats, while the warm Jurassic seas teemed with **plankton**, which fed large fish such as *Leedsichthys*. Giant sea turtles weighing 4,500 pounds (2,041 kg) lived in a Jurassic ocean that covered what is now the state of Wyoming. In other Jurassic seas, there were abundant coral reefs, fish, **ichthyosaurs**, giant marine crocodiles, and the first sharklike animals. *Archaeopteryx*, the first primitive bird, appeared during the last five million years of *Stegosaurus*'s time on Earth. There were also many flying reptiles called pterosaurs, which were the largest **vertebrates** ever known to fly.

Dinosaurs grew enormous during the Middle and Late Jurassic. They also produced a greater variety of species and spread around the globe. The Jurassic Period was the golden age of the long-necked herbivorous dinosaurs known as sauropods. *Stegosaurus* walked among many friendly plant-eaters such as heavyweights *Diplodocus*, *Apatosaurus*, and *Brachiosaurus*. But there were meat-eating predators such as the multi-ton killers *Allosaurus*, *Ceratosaurus*, and *Torvosaurus* lurking in the forests. A typical Jurassic

food chain began with low-lying vegetation, continued with an herbivorous *Stegosaurus*, and ended with an *Allosaurus*.

Allosaurus and *Ceratosaurus*, both bipedal theropods, were probably the greatest dangers to *Stegosaurus*. If attacked, *Stegosaurus* would have stood its ground, pivoted, and whipped its war club of a tail to puncture the throat and cripple any charging attacker. The vicious meat-eaters would have lunged for the unprotected belly of the well-armored *Stegosaurus*. Such a dinosaur fight would have been an awesome display of strength. Packs of smaller theropods may have also preyed on *Stegosaurus* by using teamwork.

Just prior to and during the Late Jurassic and Early Cretaceous periods (from about 161 to 100 million years ago), stegosaurs became quite diverse, with different species displaying a wide variety of spikes and plates. Although *Stegosaurus* has been found only in North America, there were many related species of stegosaur living in Africa, Europe, and Asia around the same time, such as *Kentrosaurus*. This African relative was half the size of *Stegosaurus* but was also well protected with spikes and plates, which ran midway along its spine to its tail. *Lexovisaurus* is the earliest known stegosaur, having lived about 160 million years ago, or 10 million years before *Stegosaurus*. Fossils of *Lexovisaurus* have been found in France and northern England and show that it was similar in size to *Stegosaurus*, but its spikes had a more pointed shape.

Vicious *Allosaurus*

The largest and most ferocious known predator of the Late Jurassic may have had *Stegosaurus* for dinner. *Allosaurus*, meaning "different lizard," was a formidable hunter equipped with powerful jaws, long teeth, and sharp claws. This swift-moving dinosaur averaged 28 feet (8.5 m) in length but could reach 40 feet (12.2 m) long. *Allosaurus* would have searched for small- to medium-sized dinosaurs for food. It most likely used its short but strong arms to draw prey toward its long teeth. Then it would have delivered a series of deep bites that caused the animal to die from blood loss. Although the huge meat-eater had sharp teeth, it could not crunch through bone or *Stegosaurus*'s plates. Instead, *Allosaurus* would have attacked and eaten the soft underbelly of *Stegosaurus*. This meant that there would have been plenty of meat left on the **carcass** for pterosaurs, smaller dinosaurs, and other scavenging animals. *Stegosaurus* must have tried to defend itself, as fossils of *Allosaurus* have been found with skeletal punctures that perfectly match the shape of a *Stegosaurus* tail spike.

Similar to *Allosaurus* in the U.S., the carnivorous *Metriacanthosaurus* (pictured) hunted stegosaur relatives in what is now England.

Around 146 million years ago, stegosaurs began to disappear. By 99 million years ago, they had become **extinct**. No one knows why. Most scientists believe that a minor mass extinction event occurred toward the end of the Jurassic Period. The huge plant-eating dinosaurs began to die out, as did many marine reptiles. The extinction, rather than wiping out whole families, simply eliminated certain species. Neither *Stegosaurus* nor any of its direct relatives survived long into the Cretaceous Period. Perhaps their food sources became scarce or a disease destroyed them.

Almost 35 million years later, all of the flying reptiles and dinosaurs disappeared during a mass extinction at the end of the Cretaceous. Many scientists believe that the cause of the mass extinction, known as the K-T (Cretaceous-Tertiary) extinction event, was probably a giant meteor that crashed into the planet 65 million years ago. The impact likely resulted in a release of hot gases and dust that filled the sky, blocking the sun and cooling the earth significantly. With plants unable to grow, the herbivores would have weakened and died out first, while the meat-eaters would have fed on the plant-eaters and then starved to death themselves. Although exactly what happened may never be known, by the beginning of the Tertiary Period 65 million years ago, all of the dinosaurs had gone the way of *Stegosaurus*.

35

PUZZLING PLATES AND ARMOR

Since *Stegosaurus stenops* was discovered in 1886, scientists have offered various theories about the armored dinosaur's physical makeup, behaviors, and habitat. Ideas about the animal's diet, too, have changed over the years. At first it was thought that *Stegosaurus* had weak teeth used to feed only on soft food; today, however, scientists believe that the dinosaur used its hard beak to nip off plants and then chewed the tough vegetation with its numerous and small triangular teeth. However, fossil evidence shows *Stegosaurus* teeth with little wear, so it may be that much of the plant material was swallowed whole. The narrow snout may also indicate that *Stegosaurus* was a selective feeder and only picked out choice items such as seed-fern "fruits" and the leaves of **cycads**, having no need to chew more complicated plant matter.

New information is constantly being discovered about stegosaurs. In 1992, the most complete *Stegosaurus* skeleton on record was discovered by paleontologists Bryan Small, Tim Seeber, and Kenneth Carpenter near the Garden Park fossil area of Colorado. They nicknamed their find "Spike." Before Spike was uncovered, scientists knew that *Stegosaurus* possessed plates but were unsure how they were arranged upon the neck, back, and tail. Some thought they had been paired. Others thought they alternated. A third group put them on one row, with big plates overlapping. Spike, the new, beautifully

Artists' depictions of *Stegosaurus* vary greatly, but some take care to show how the dinosaur may have grasped its leafy food with its beak.

preserved skeleton, finally proved that the 17 plates had formed two rows alternating in alignment. It was also determined for the first time that disk-shaped plates protected *Stegosaurus*'s hips and the soft area under its throat.

As for the back plates' purpose, paleontologists first thought that they were to prevent predators from jumping on top of *Stegosaurus*. However, it is now also known that a honeycomb pattern of blood veins ran throughout the skin that covered the plates, helping to regulate the dinosaur's body temperature. Some scientists think that if *Stegosaurus* stood sideways to the morning sun, the blood in its sun-warmed plates grew hotter and energized the animal's body. If *Stegosaurus* stood with its back to the scorching midday rays, the sun did not strike the flat surface of the plates, which shed more heat than they gained. Similar to the way an elephant flaps its ears to cool off, the **asymmetrical** arrangement of the plates would also have helped *Stegosaurus* lose heat to the air, whatever the direction of the wind.

Today, in addition to the plates' defensive properties, most scientists think that the bizarre body armor of *Stegosaurus* probably served as an extreme example of the elaborate and colorful displays some animals use to recognize mates. The plates, also called osteoderms, originated from under the skin, similar to lizard scales. During mating season, a male *Stegosaurus* may have been able to move the hard plates on its back to attract a mate or intimidate

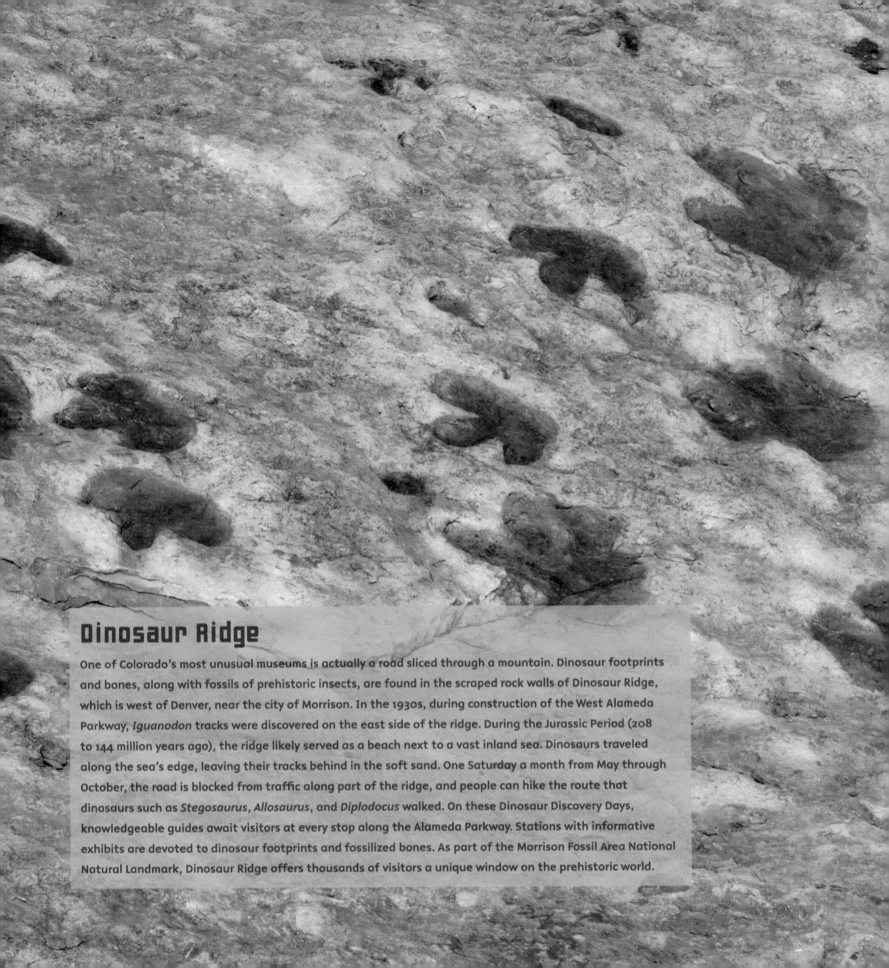

Dinosaur Ridge

One of Colorado's most unusual museums is actually a road sliced through a mountain. Dinosaur footprints and bones, along with fossils of prehistoric insects, are found in the scraped rock walls of Dinosaur Ridge, which is west of Denver, near the city of Morrison. In the 1930s, during construction of the West Alameda Parkway, *Iguanodon* tracks were discovered on the east side of the ridge. During the Jurassic Period (208 to 144 million years ago), the ridge likely served as a beach next to a vast inland sea. Dinosaurs traveled along the sea's edge, leaving their tracks behind in the soft sand. One Saturday a month from May through October, the road is blocked from traffic along part of the ridge, and people can hike the route that dinosaurs such as *Stegosaurus*, *Allosaurus*, and *Diplodocus* walked. On these Dinosaur Discovery Days, knowledgeable guides await visitors at every stop along the Alameda Parkway. Stations with informative exhibits are devoted to dinosaur footprints and fossilized bones. As part of the Morrison Fossil Area National Natural Landmark, Dinosaur Ridge offers thousands of visitors a unique window on the prehistoric world.

Monumental Fossils

Dinosaur National Monument is located in a remote part of northwestern Colorado and eastern Utah where there are high sandstone cliffs and the valleys of the Green and Yampa rivers. Inside the monument's boundaries is the quarry that produced the largest single collection of bones from the Jurassic Period. U.S. president Woodrow Wilson proclaimed the great dinosaur quarry a national monument in 1915. The area's main attraction was a steep cliff face that formed a massive wall in the Quarry Visitor Center and included nearly 2,000 bones from dinosaurs such as *Stegosaurus*, *Diplodocus*, and *Camptosaurus*. After being closed for foundation repair since July 2006, the center was set to reopen in 2011. In the meantime, visitors could see dinosaur specimens in a temporary center and hike the Fossil Discovery Trail. Because of the large concentration of bones in one place, scientists believe the area once contained an ancient dinosaur watering hole. Eventually, the dinosaurs died and were fossilized under layers of sand and gravel. After ages of rain and wind, the long-buried bones surfaced. Paleontologist Earl Douglass found the site in 1909 when he discovered eight segments of an *Apatosaurus* tail.

a competitor. Muscles connected to bone may have allowed the dinosaur to flap the plates back and forth.

One of the controversies that has long surrounded *Stegosaurus* and its brain size is still being debated. In the late 1880s, O. C. Marsh set forth a theory that *Stegosaurus* had two brains. When Marsh obtained a well-preserved *Stegosaurus* skull and made a cast, or model, of it, he concluded that the dinosaur's brain was the smallest among dinosaurs. Soon after, he noted a spinal cord enlargement in the hip region of *Stegosaurus*. This space could have accommodated a structure up to 20 times larger than the dinosaur's walnut-sized brain and led to a widespread belief that *Stegosaurus* may have had a "second brain" in the tail to control the animal's hindquarters. Recently, relying on studies performed by paleontologists such as Kenneth Carpenter at the Denver Museum of Nature and Science, most scientists reject the "second brain theory" and concur that the enlarged area in the hip consisted of nerve cells or fatty tissue that may have helped control movement or stored carbohydrates to supply energy to the nervous system.

Scientists also continue to speculate about whether *Stegosaurus* lived in groups or by themselves. Tracks discovered by Matthew Mossbrucker of the Morrison Natural History Museum in Morrison, Colorado, suggest that *Stegosaurus* lived in multi-age herds. The

Although more is now known about *Stegosaurus*'s skull, other research continues to be carried out at sites such as the quarry in Dinosaur National Monument.

tracks discovered in the Morrison Formation, an area of sedimentary rock that dates from the Late Jurassic, show baby, juvenile, and adult *Stegosaurus* all intermingled with each other. Through his fossil studies in Colorado, Robert Bakker, **curator** of paleontology for the Houston Museum of Natural Sciences, has also put forth new evidence that not all Jurassic dinosaurs lived in the same kinds of areas. He has proven through locations of fossil finds that *Stegosaurus* herds were present only on well-drained, dry soil.

Bakker has also researched one of Edward Drinker Cope's greatest theories. Cope theorized that some prehistoric animals grew bigger and bigger until they eventually died out. Bakker and other scientists believe that dinosaurs such as *Stegosaurus* were creatures that became too big and clumsy to fend for themselves, falling prey to agile predators or becoming unable to eat enough food to sustain themselves. They then died out.

Much has changed in paleontology since 1886, when Marshall Felch dug up the *Stegosaurus* skull that completed the first skeleton of the species. Many of the old, painstaking fossil-finding methods have been replaced by technological advances such as power tools that can remove the surplus rock around ancient fossils. And computers

Marsh's Top Five

In the mid-1800s, O. C. Marsh recorded a 15-step procedure for collecting fossils. Following are the first five instructions on the list:

1. On leaving camp to collect, always take proper tools, and also sacks, paper cotton and twine, so as to pack specimens where found. Otherwise they may be badly injured in getting them to the camp.

2. The best way to find fossils is to go over all the ground on foot, slowly and carefully. Haste makes waste in collecting, as the best specimens may easily be overlooked.

3. It is of the greatest importance to keep the bones of each animal by themselves, separate from all the others, and to save all the pieces, however small or weathered.

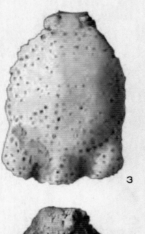

4. Collect carefully all the loose bones and fragments, on the surface or covered with earth, before beginning to dig out the rest of the skeleton. Otherwise valuable pieces are sure to be lost.

5. Never remove all the rock from a skull, foot, or other delicate specimen. The more valuable the fossil, the more rock should be left to protect it. Better send 100 pounds [45.4 kg] of rock, than leave a tool mark on a good specimen.

can now reconstruct dinosaurs' bone structure and simulate their movement. However, removing and restoring dinosaur bones remains a time-consuming and labor-intensive process today.

As *Stegosaurus* specimens and other dinosaur and reptile fossils continue to be uncovered and studied, any new details about a species bring scientists closer to understanding what life on Earth was like millions of years ago. More than 100 years after the first stegosaur fossils were discovered, scientists are still learning more about them and their reptilian relatives. And a century from now, they will probably have still more to discover.

Paleontologists and fossil hunters spend years researching and collecting bones in hopes of being able to recreate partial or complete skeletons.

Stegosaurus compared with a five-foot-tall (152 cm) human

46

GLOSSARY

asymmetrical—having parts that are not equal or correspondingly placed

carcass—the dead body of an animal

carnivorous—describing an animal that feeds on other animals

chain mail—flexible body armor made of small metal rings linked together

climate—the long-term weather conditions of an area

clutch—a group of eggs produced and developed at the same time

conifers—evergreen trees, such as pines and firs, that bear cones

curator—the person in charge of a museum or art collection

cycads—tropical palmlike plants that bear large cones

embryos—organisms in the early stages of development before they emerge from the egg

evolve—to adapt or change over time to survive in a certain environment

extinct—having no living members

food chain—a system in nature in which living things are dependent on each other for food

herbivores—animals that feed only on plants

ichthyosaurs—giant marine reptiles resembling fish and dolphins that thrived throughout the Mesozoic Era (245 to 65 million years ago)

mammals—warm-blooded animals that have a backbone and hair or fur, give birth to live young, and produce milk to feed their young

medieval—pertaining to the Middle Ages, a period of European history that lasted from about A.D 400 to 1500

paleontologists—scientists who study fossilized plants and animals

plankton—the small or microscopic plant and animal organisms that float or drift in the water

reptiles—cold-blooded animals with scaly skin that typically lay eggs on land

species—a group of living organisms that share similar characteristics and can mate with one another

vertebrates—animals that have a backbone, or spinal column

SELECTED BIBLIOGRAPHY

Fastovsky, David, and David Weishampel. *The Evolution and Extinction of the Dinosaurs*. Cambridge: Cambridge University Press, 2005.

Haines, Tim, and Paul Chambers. *The Complete Guide to Prehistoric Life*. Buffalo, N.Y.: Firefly Books, 2007.

Lambert, David. *The Ultimate Dinosaur Book*. New York: DK Publishing, 1993.

Psihoyos, Louie, and John Knoebber. *Hunting Dinosaurs*. New York: Random House, 1994.

Rajewski, Genevieve. "Where Dinosaurs Roamed." *Smithsonian Magazine*, 39, no. 2 (May, 2008): 20–24.

Wallace, David. *The Bonehunters' Revenge*. Boston: Mariner Books, 2000.

INDEX

READ MORE

Barrett, Paul. *National Geographic Dinosaurs*. Washington, D.C.: National Geographic Society, 2001.

Gee, Henry, and Luis V. Rey. *A Field Guide to Dinosaurs*. Boston: Barron's, 2003.

Holz, Thomas R., and Luis V. Rey. *Dinosaurs: the Most Complete, Up-to-Date Encyclopedia for Dinosaur Lovers of All Ages*. New York: Random House, 2007.

Jaffe, Mark. *The Gilded Dinosaur: The Fossil War Between E. D. Cope and O. C. Marsh and the Rise of American Science*. New York: Three Rivers Press, 2001.

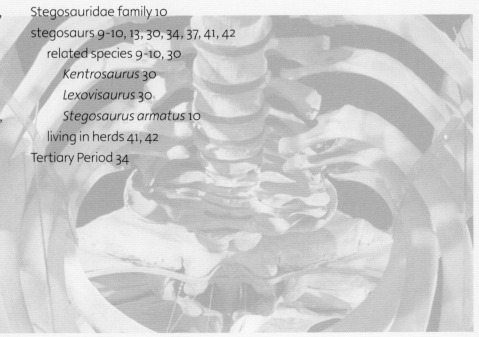